Hector P. Garcia Middle School
14900 Kyle Seale Parkway
San Antonio, Texas 78255

LIBRARY OF WEIRD

# THE WORLD'S
# WEIRDEST
# ANIMALS

by Lindsy O'Brien

CAPSTONE PRESS
a capstone imprint

Edge Books are published by Capstone Press,
1710 Roe Crest Drive, North Mankato, Minnesota 56003.
www.capstonepub.com

**Library of Congress Cataloging-in-Publication Data**
O'Brien, Lindsy, author.
The world's weirdest animals / by Lindsy O'Brien.
pages cm.—(Edge books. Library of weird)
Summary: "Describes some of the weirdest, craziest, and oddest animals from around
the world"—Provided by publisher.
Includes bibliographical references and index.
ISBN 978-1-4914-2019-5 (library binding)
ISBN 978-1-4914-2190-1 (ebook PDF)
1. Animals—Miscellanea—Juvenile literature. I. Title.
QL49.O27 2015
590.2—dc23                                    2014013941

**Editorial Credits**
Aaron Sautter, editor; Kyle Grenz, designer; Charmaine Whitman and Katy
LaVigne, production designers; Pam Mitsakos, media researcher; Kathy McColley,
production specialist

**Photo Credits**
Dreamstime: Smellme, 10; Getty Images: Photodisc, 29 (bottom); Minden Pictures:
Norbert Wu, 17; Nature Picture Library: Solvin Zankl, 16; Newscom: "CMSP
Biology", 11, Minden Pictures/FLPA/Dembinsky Photo Ass, 8, ZUMAPRESS/Kerryn
Parkinson, 13, Visual&Written, 15; Shutterstock: BMJ, 21, Erni, 29 (top), gallimaufry,
7, Sue Green, 26, Arto Hakola, 9, cover, Eric Isselee, 5, Nataly Karol, 18, Steve
Lovegrove, back cover, Molly Marshall, 25, Dudarev Mikhail, 19, 24, nattanan726,
27, orlandin, 14, Yakov Oskanov, 6, Peter Reijners, 23, reptiles4all, 28, Michael
Wiggenhauser, 20; Wikimedia:Darron Birgenheier, 22

**Design Elements**
Shutterstock: AridOcean, KID_A (throughout)

Printed in the United States of America in Stevens Point, Wisconsin.
092014    008479WZS15

# TABLE OF CONTENTS

# WEIRD AND WACKY
# ANIMALS

Do you know about ocean fish that look like blobs of goo or glow like flashlights? Have you heard about antelope that can stand on their hind legs? What about a chicken that looks like it should be wearing a scarf?

From bugs to birds, animals around the world have a wide variety of weird characteristics. Some animals look freaky and strange while others show bizarre behavior. But being different often helps them survive in the wild. Some animals have bright colors or act strangely to scare off **predators**. Other animals have odd body shapes that help them get food that others can't reach.

predator—*an animal that hunts other animals for food*

Weird animals are found around the world. From the air, to the land, to the sea, and even in outer space, outlandish creatures can be found wherever you look. Get ready to meet some crazy creatures you have to see to believe.

# OKAPI

Okapis are rare relatives of giraffes. Though smaller, they have a similar body shape to giraffes. But unlike giraffes, these animals have zebralike stripes on their hindquarters and front legs. Okapis have tongues up to 14 inches (36 centimeters) long. They use their long tongues to grab leaves and shoots from tall branches. Okapis are rarely seen in the wild. For a long time people thought the animals were a myth. For this reason they long carried the nickname "African unicorns."

# CHAPTER 1
# MYSTERIOUS MAMMALS

You may already be familiar with many *mammals*. Common animals such as cats, dogs, horses, deer, and others are all mammals. But some of the world's weirdest animals are mammals too.

## FLYING FOX

The flying fox isn't a fox at all—it's a bat! But its furry face and big eyes make it look similar to a fox. Most bats eat insects, but flying foxes are **vegetarians**. They make meals out of **nectar**, pollen, and fruits. Flying foxes live in several tropical areas around the world.

## SAIGA ANTELOPE

Saiga antelope roam the plains of Central Asia. These animals once numbered in the millions, but today there are only about 150,000 of them in the wild. Saiga antelopes have large humped noses that help control the temperature of the air they breathe. This ability helps the animals survive extreme hot and cold temperatures in winter and summer.

# TARSIER

Tarsiers live in Southeast Asia. These small creatures grow only about 4 to 6 inches (10 to 15 cm) long. They eat mostly insects, but sometimes they eat lizards or small birds as well. Tarsiers have giant eyes that help them see their prey in the dark. These creatures can also turn their heads half way around their bodies to see what's directly behind them!

**mammal**—*a warm-blooded animal that breathes air; mammals feed milk to their young*

**vegetarian**—*an animal or person who does not eat meat*

**nectar**—*a sweet liquid found in many flowers*

# HOODED SEAL

The noses of male hooded seals can blow up like red balloons. Male seals use their red noses to threaten other males during mating season. Hooded seals live in northern parts of the Atlantic Ocean.

# STAR-NOSED MOLE

North American star-nosed moles have 25,000 sensory nerves on their noses. The moles' sensitive noses help them find food in wetlands and marshes. While underwater these animals often blow bubbles from their noses and suck them back in. Scientists believe the bubbles trap odors to help moles sniff out their surroundings while underwater.

# NAKED MOLE RAT

Is it an alien? Maybe it's a baby hairless squirrel. No, this **rodent** is called the naked mole rat. Its huge tusklike front teeth are used for digging tunnels underground. The mole rat lives underground in the dark and is nearly blind. It feels its way through tunnels using tiny hairs on its body.

**rodent**—*a mammal with long front teeth used for gnawing*

# DUCK-BILLED PLATYPUS

Australia's duck-billed platypus is one of the world's only poisonous mammals. The male has a clawlike spine on its ankle that carries **venom**. The platypus is also one of the few mammals in the world that lays eggs. This strange animal closes its eyes, ears, and nostrils when it hunts and swims underwater. The platypus hunts instead with its highly sensitive bill that can easily detect the movements of nearby fish.

**venom**—*poisonous liquid produced by some animals*

# LOWLAND STREAKED TENREC

The lowland streaked tenrec looks like a hairy yellow and black mouse. But this tiny creature is actually more like a porcupine. It can defend itself with quills that can detach and stick to predators. It can also rub special quills together to make a high-pitched noise that scares off predators. The tenrec is one of many animals found only in Madagascar.

## AYE-AYE

Aye-ayes are some of the strangest-looking creatures in the world. They have large batlike ears, bushy tails, long fingers, and large eyes to see in the dark. Aye-ayes look so bizarre that some people in Madagascar believe the animals are a sign of bad luck. They believe that aye-ayes should be killed on sight. There are fewer than 10,000 of these odd creatures left in the world.

## SLENDER LORIS

The slender loris was named for the Dutch word meaning "clown." It has giant eyes to help it see in the dark. In fact, the loris' eyes are so big that they take up as much room in the animal's skull as its brain! The loris lives only on the island of Sri Lanka.

## PYGMY MARMOSET

The pygmy marmoset lives in South America and is the world's smallest monkey. It grows only about as big as a human hand. However, it can leap up to 16 feet (4.9 meters) between rain forest trees!

# EMPEROR TAMARIN

The South American emperor tamarin is a small species of monkey. It is supposedly named after Germany's Emperor Wilhelm II. This is due to the tamarin's long white moustache. It looks very similar to how Wilhelm II's moustache looked.

# PINK FAIRY ARMADILLO

What is pink, weighs less than 1 pound (0.5 kilogram), and moves through sand as if it were swimming in water? The pink fairy armadillo! This creature lives in Argentina. It easily moves through sand because its front feet work like shovels. The armadillo also has a tiny pointed head that helps it wedge its way into small spaces.

# CHAPTER 2
# ODD OCEAN CREATURES

The world's oceans can be a dangerous place to live. Still, they are home to a huge variety of animal life. Each ocean animal has unique traits and behaviors to survive—and some of them are totally bizarre!

## GOBLIN SHARK

The goblin shark has been called "the ugliest living shark." Its long snout looks like a visor above its eyes. Nobody is sure what the long snout is for. Some scientists think the sharks use their snouts to detect electrical signals from other fish. When the goblin shark's mouth is open, it looks very much like a toothy goblin.

## YETI CRAB

Yeti crabs are white and hairy and grow to about the size of a human hand. Scientists think the crabs' silky hairs may help trap the bacteria that they eat. Yeti crabs live near **hydrothermal vents** on the ocean floor to stay warm.

**hydrothermal vent**—*a hot spring on the ocean floor*

## BLUE SEA SLUG

The blue sea slug often floats on the ocean surface to find food. This creature is a master of disguise. One side of the slug is silvery gray to help it hide from sea creatures below it. The other side of the slug's body is colored blue to help it hide from birds in the air.

## TRIPOD FISH

The tripod fish doesn't bother chasing after its prey. It instead props itself up on the ocean floor with three tall, stiltlike fins. Then it simply stands in place and waits for prey to come close enough to catch.

## BLOBFISH

The blobfish has been called the world's most miserable-looking fish and voted to be the world's ugliest animal. This fish looks just like its name—a big, ugly blob. Scientists believe this creature spends most of its time bobbing in the water waiting for food to float by.

## HAIRY FROGFISH

The hairy frogfish attracts prey by wiggling a fleshy arm above its forehead like a fishing pole. This predator can stretch its mouth up to 12 times its normal size to swallow prey whole. These bizarre fish can also change color to blend in with their surroundings.

## PINK HANDFISH

The pink handfish of Tasmania walks on its fins instead of swimming. Its fins are shaped much like human hands, which is how the fish got its name. These slow-moving fish are extremely rare. Only four of them have ever been found, and none have been seen since 1999.

# RED-LIPPED BATFISH

Sometimes even fish seem to try to keep up with fashion trends. For example, the red-lipped batfish looks like it put on too much lipstick. The batfish lives near the Galapagos Islands and doesn't swim. It instead uses its back fins to "walk" across the ocean floor.

# SQUAT LOBSTER

Squat lobsters look similar to lobsters, but are actually related to crabs. Their arms and claws often grow several times as long as their bodies. Some small types of squat lobsters on Australia's coral reef look like colorful plastic toys.

## DUMBO OCTOPUS

The tiny Dumbo octopus usually grows only 8 to 10 inches (20 to 25 cm) tall. It was named for the two fins on top of its head. When it flaps its fins, it looks similar to the flying elephant from the movie *Dumbo*.

## GIANT ISOPODS

Some animals grow much bigger in deep oceans than on land. This effect is called deep sea gigantism. Most land isopods, such as pillbugs, grow only about 0.5 inch (1.3 cm) long. But giant isopods in deep seas can grow up to 15 inches (38 cm) long!

# ANGLERFISH

The anglerfish could also be called the "angry fish." It always looks cranky. But it got its name from the fleshy spine that sticks out from its head. This spine looks like a fishing pole and has a glowing tip to lure in prey.

# BARRELEYE FISH

Some fish live so deep in the ocean that they're hardly ever seen. One of the strangest of these is the barreleye fish. Its barrel-shaped eyes are found inside its glowing, see-through head. It usually looks up through its head to watch for prey. But it can also roll its eyes forward to find and catch its food.

# CHAPTER 3

# BIZARRE BUGS AND BIRDS

The world is full of weird birds and bugs. Whether it's flightless parrots or worms that glow in the dark, you can find bizarre bugs and birds no matter where you travel.

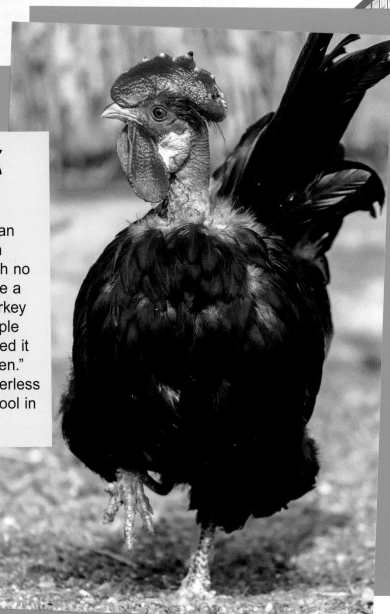

## NAKED NECK CHICKEN

The Transylvanian naked neck chicken has a long neck with no feathers. It looks like a cross between a turkey and a chicken. People have even nicknamed it a "churkey" or "turken." The chicken's featherless neck helps it stay cool in hot temperatures.

## GIRAFFE WEEVIL

The male giraffe weevil has a long hinged neck that acts like a crane. Male weevils use their necks to fight other males for a mate. Females also have long necks, but they are much shorter than males. Females use their necks to roll up leaves to create nests for their eggs. These beetles are found only in the forests of Madagascar.

## ELEPHANT HAWK MOTH

The elephant hawk moth is found in North America and in northern regions of Europe and Asia. It is one of the fastest animals in the world. This big moth can fly up to 30 miles (48 kilometers) per hour! It can also hover and change direction quickly like a hummingbird. The caterpillar of this moth is long and gray like an elephant's trunk.

## PANDA ANT

The panda ant is found in Chile. It looks like an ant dressed up in a panda suit. However, it's not really an ant at all. It's actually a type of black and white wingless wasp. Also known as "cow killer" ants, these wasps have painful stings. They are said to be powerful enough to kill a cow.

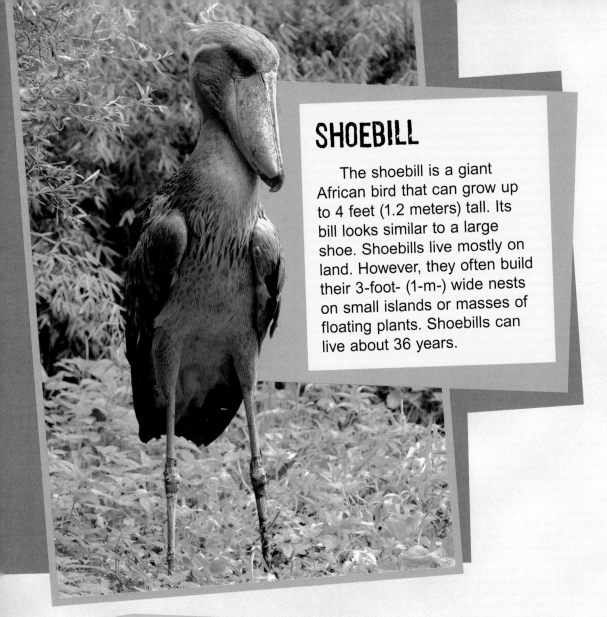

## SHOEBILL

The shoebill is a giant African bird that can grow up to 4 feet (1.2 meters) tall. Its bill looks similar to a large shoe. Shoebills live mostly on land. However, they often build their 3-foot- (1-m-) wide nests on small islands or masses of floating plants. Shoebills can live about 36 years.

## NORTHERN SHRIKE

Northern shrikes look like harmless songbirds. However, they are fierce hunters and are often called "butcher birds." These birds kill more prey than they eat at one time. They often store the extra food for later. Sometimes they stab their prey onto thorns or barbed wire while it's still alive. Northern shrikes eat insects, small mammals and birds, and sometimes reptiles.

# KAKAPO PARROT

The world's heaviest parrot weighs up to 9 pounds (4.1 kg) and can't fly. Kakapo parrots instead climb trees and glide back to the ground. These colorful birds smell like honey because of a type of harmless bacteria that live on their feathers. The kakapo is found on only a few islands in New Zealand.

# BOWERBIRD

Bowerbirds live in New Guinea and Australia. They make large nests called bowers out of sticks and twigs. Some bowerbird nests look like two tall, connected towers. Bowerbirds often decorate their nests with colorful objects. The satin bowerbird often uses brightly colored trash and objects made of blue plastic in its nest.

# TARDIGRADES

Found all over the world, tardigrades are the ultimate survivors. These **microscopic** creatures are often known as "water bears." Their bodies have tough outer coverings that help them survive in even the most difficult conditions. These little critters can live for years without water and can even survive in outer space!

**microscopic**—*too small to be seen without a microscope*

# ARMY ANTS

Army ants protect their queen and her eggs by creating **bivouacs**. The ants make these shelters by packing their bodies tightly together. Many species of army ants live in Central and South America. They are aggressive meat eaters. Army ants are known to form dangerous swarms to attack prey and predators.

**bivouac**—*a temporary shelter*

# GLOWWORMS

If you see thousands of glittering lights on a cave wall, it might be glowworm **larvae**. Adult glowworm insects create light to help attract mates. The larvae also glow, but they create light to attract and trap prey. They're often found in caves in Australia and New Zealand.

**larvae**—insects at the stage of development between an egg and an adult

# DRAGON-HEADED KATYDID

Borneo's dragon-headed katydid is the size of a large grasshopper. This colorful bug looks like it's wearing too much makeup. It has bulging blue eyes and a bright pink face. The katydid also has an extremely loud and high-pitched mating call.

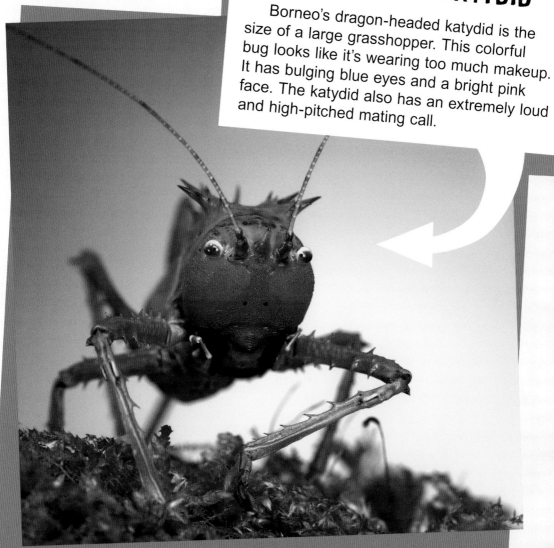

# CHAPTER 4

# UNUSUAL ADAPTATIONS

From deserts to rain forests, there are many different *habitats*. Animals often make their homes in some of the toughest places on Earth. Animals in these locations have to *adapt* to survive. Some animals have gone through extreme changes and may seem like strange creatures from another world.

## MANED WOLF

The maned wolf of South America has very long, slender legs that help it step over tall plants and grasses. The wolf also has 7-inch- (18-cm-) long ears. The maned wolf may look large and frightening, but it's actually very timid. It eats a mix of small animals and tropical plants such as bananas.

**habitat**—*the natural place and conditions in which an animal lives*

**adapt**—*to change in order to survive*

## FOSSA

Would you like to run into a "killing machine"? That's what people in Madagascar call the fossa. These odd creatures have specialized feet and claws. They can easily climb up and down trees going headfirst in either direction. This ability makes fossas excellent hunters. They eat mostly lemurs, rodents, and reptiles. But they sometimes hunt farm animals such as chickens and goats. Although fossas look similar to cats, they are actually a type of mongoose.

# SUN BEAR

The world's smallest bear lives in Southeast Asia. The sun bear grows to weigh only about 150 pounds (68 kg). The sun bear gets its name from the patch of gold or white hair on its chest. Some people think this patch resembles a rising sun. Sun bears have an especially long tongue that grows to nearly 10-inches (25-cm) long. They use their tongues to reach insects, grubs, and honey inside trees.

# GERENUK ANTELOPE

The gerenuk antelope can stand on two legs to eat! It does this to reach its long neck into trees to eat leaves and shoots. It gets all the moisture it needs from its food. The gerenuk can live its whole life without drinking water.

# INDIA PURPLE FROG

Is a frog still a frog if it can't jump? The India purple frog has short back legs. Although it can move with long strides, it can't leap. This weird frog comes above ground for only 2 to 3 weeks a year during mating season. It grows up to 2.7 inches (7 cm) long.

# TADPOLE SHRIMP

Tadpole shrimp eggs can lie **dormant** in clay for years. The eggs hatch only when heavy rains finally come. The shrimp grow up in the mud, lay new eggs, and die within a few days of hatching. The new eggs will wait to hatch for the next big rain. Different types of tadpole shrimp are found all over the world.

**dormant**—*not active*

# THORNY DEVIL

Australia's thorny devil could easily be mistaken for a tiny dragon. This lizard's sharp spines are put to good use. The spines make it difficult for predators to swallow these lizards. Dew also gathers on the spines at night so the lizard has water to drink. Thorny devils also have spiny lumps on their backs that look like a second head. When threatened by a predator, the lizard ducks its head so only the spiny, fake head is seen. The lizard's fake head provides good protection from predators.

# FENNEC FOX

The fennec fox is the smallest fox in the world. At only about 10- to 16-inches (25- to 41-cm) long—the fox is smaller than most house cats. But this little fox has giant ears that grow up to 6-inches (15 cm) long. The fox's big ears help keep it cool in the heat of Africa's Sahara Desert. Fennec foxes also have hairy feet that act like snowshoes to keep them from sinking into the sand.

# ELECTRIC FISH

Electric fish live in freshwater lakes and rivers in Africa and South America. Electric fish send weak electrical pulses through the water to communicate with one another. Some of these fish can produce enough electricity to stun their prey. Electric eels, for example, can produce up to 600 volts of electricity. That's five times stronger than the electricity in most U.S. homes!

# GHARIAL

The gharial of India is one of the world's biggest crocodiles. It can reach 20 to 23 feet (6 to 7 m) in length, which is longer than most cars! It has a round bulb on the tip of its narrow nose called a ghara. This bulb is used to make a very loud buzzing or hissing noise during mating season.

# DESERT JERBOA

The desert jerboa needs very little water. It can survive on the water found in its food. The jerboa has fur on the bottom of its feet to keep it from sinking into the sand. Like the fennec fox, the jerboa's large ears give off heat to keep its body cool in the deserts of northern Africa.

# AXOLOTL

The ocean isn't the only place strange water animals call home. The axolotl is an **amphibian** that lives in just one lake in Mexico. The axolotl spends its whole life in water. But unlike frogs or toads, it doesn't lose its gills or tail as it gets older.

**amphibian**—*a cold blooded animal with a backbone; amphibians live in water when young and usually live on land as adults*

# A WORLD OF WEIRD WILDLIFE

Some animals look or act strange. But they usually have good reasons for their odd appearance or behavior. Being different can be a good thing. Unique traits often help animals survive in the wild. Weird and bizarre animals are found all around us. Keep your eyes open—you never know when you might see one near you!

# GLOSSARY

**adapt** (uh-DAPT)—to change in order to survive

**amphibian** (am-FI-bee-uhn)—a cold-blooded animal with a backbone; amphibians live in water when young and usually live on land as adults

**bivouac** (BIV-oo-ak)—a temporary shelter

**dormant** (DOR-muhnt)—not active

**habitat** (HAB-uh-tat)—the natural place and conditions in which an animal lives

**hydrothermal vent** (hi-dro-THUR-muhl VENT)—a hot spring on the ocean floor

**larvae** (LAR-vay)—insects at the stage of development between an egg and an adult

**mammal** (MAM-uhl)—a warm-blooded animal that breathes air, mammals feed milk to their young

**microscopic** (mye-kruh-SKOP-ik)—too small to be seen without a microscope

**nectar** (NEK-tur)—a sweet liquid found in many flowers

**predator** (PRED-uh-tur)—an animal that hunts other animals for food

**prey** (PRAY)—an animal hunted by another animal for food

**rodent** (ROH-duhnt)—a mammal with long front teeth used for gnawing

**vegetarian** (vej-uh-TER-ee-uhn)—an animal or person who does not eat meat

**venom** (VEN-uhm)—poisonous liquid produced by some animals

# READ MORE

**Montgomery, Heather.** *Wild Discoveries: Wacky New Animals.*
New York: Scholastic, 2013.

**Peterson, Megan Cooley**. *This Book Might Bite: A Collection
of Wacky Animal Trivia.* Super Trivia Collection. North Mankato,
Minn.: Capstone Press, 2012.

**Spelman, Lucy.** *National Geographic Animal Encyclopedia.*
Washington, D.C.: National Geographic, 2012.

# INTERNET SITES

FactHound offers a safe, fun way to find Internet sites
related to this book. All of the sites on FactHound have
been researched by our staff.

Here's all you do:

Visit *www.facthound.com*

Type in this code: 9781491420195

# INDEX